Robert Garnham is a spoken word artist, originally from Surrey, now based in Devon. He has performed all over the UK at some of the top spoken word nights, festivals and fringes.

Nice (2015) *Burning Eye*
Reception (2016) *Soulsoaker Books*
Zebra (2017) *Burning Eye*
Yak (2018) *Puddlehopper Books*
Spout (2019) *Puddlehopper Books*

This edition published by Puddlehopper Books 2020
www.professorofwhimsy.com

@RobertGarnham

Puddlehopper Books
Paignton, Devon

ISBN
979-8-695-15434-4

Squidbox

Robert Garnham

Puddlehopper Books

SQUIDBOX ROBERT GARNHAM

The Trawler Basin
A Scream for the Sea
Hive of Activity on the Hottest Day of the Year
Why Have Most of the Boats Got Feminine Names?
Margaret of Ladram Leaves the Quay
Thirty Years Man and Boy
Solo Skipper
Tristan
Rough
General Synopsis
Sunrise
Interview with a Trawlerman
Poet in Residence on a Beam Trawler
The Sea Monster
The Ghost Ships
It's Just What You Do In This Town
This Is My Life
The Skipper's Decision
Sometimes They Don't Come Back
Dan
I Want to Be a Skipper
Do You Hear the Sea Still Calling?
The Battle of the Eastern Scruff
Mum Ruled the Roost
Ther Fish Hawkers
Little Ostend
Squidbox
Seagrasses
Biodiversity
I Don't Know Much About Marine Biology
I'm a Trawler
The Fish Market has Gone Online
All-Night Humming from the Ice Factory
I Like It Here
We are Brixham
Homecoming

In 1996 I moved with my parents from Surrey to Brixham. My parents had come down to Brixham during the 1960s for various holidays and they had always loved the place and its people. They had always said that they wanted to retire there. I came with them, and the whole place felt like a different world. I immediately fell in love with the history of the fishing industry and the traditions of those families who had a long association with the sea.

I moved away from Brixham in the year 2000, but I have continued to visit every single weekend, using the room at the back of my parent's garage as a makeshift rehearsal room as my career as a comedy performance poet grew. When the chance came to write some poems on a themed idea, funded by Torbay Culture through the Arts Council, I jumped at the chance to learn more about the Brixham fishing industry and the people who work within it.

With the help of Clare Parker, my producer, I was able to infiltrate this world. I spent a little bit of time on a trawler, (in the harbour, though; we didn't go anywhere!), and I interviewed trawlermen and people associated with the industry, as well as locals to get their view on what the fishing industry meant to them. I was also able to go behind the scenes at Brixham Museum and chat with Anna Kisby Compton, the curator, about the role that women played in the history of the fishing industry. I was also deeply inspired by Samantha Little's book, 'Battling Onwards : The Brixham Fishing Fleet 1914-1918', published by Brixham Museum. I also spent some preparation time chatting with John Hegley, a much more accomplished comedy performance poet, who gave me some ideas on how to approach the project, and who suggested poems I might read or listen to by way of inspiration. Finally, I chatted with Maggie Duffy, Brixham-based singer and songwriter, whose extensive knowledge and understanding of the town and its people were invaluable.

I hope you enjoy these poems. They don't take themselves too seriously, and they only scratch the surface of Brixham's character and history.

This second edition was devised towards the end of 2020. After the project had finished, the town was hit by the tragic sinking of the Joanna C claiming the lives of two of her crew. Two new poems have been added which reflect on this event.'

'These beautifully written, meticulously researched poems salute the pride, the passion, the craft, the history, the bravery of Brixham's fishing industry and show a deep sensitivity to and instinctive fellowship with a community that has shaped this town over many generations. Poignant, without being in the least sentimental; earthly, playful and accessible, but ambitious in ideas and dazzling in their use of language; at times, sombrely, tenderly reflective, at others seasoned with a saucy seaside humour, these poems are as salty, powerful and ever-shifting as the sea itself and get right to the heart of this fascinating, vital, but dwindling and threatened industry'

- Melanie Branton, poet

THE TRAWLER BASIN

That tangle of beams and nets and ropes
Might well be mistaken for a metal arboretum but
There are no robot squirrels here.
You!, caged whales in a concrete dock,
Shackled together as slaves on a swell,
You're nodding your bows as if each
An adventurer's remembrance of
Channel fog, white horses, force six storms,
The biggest, toughest load you ever hauled

As callous hands winch and yank, at one
With the rolling seas, you, with your
Portholes perhaps pining for the quay's embrace,
Where gathered your beams tower and peer
Like giraffes from their zoo enclosure, you,
Named for wives, girlfriends, daughters, fathers,
Ungainly, cormorants with wings folded, oh,
I think I've run out of metaphors now.

A morning's diesel throb cast off you'll seek
Invisible bounty by sonar glow, hands numbed
By cold clutching metal cups at the wheel,
How many souls have stroked your innards and
Uttered a silent trawlerman's prayer?
Keep us safe, return us once more, I have a
Life and a bank account and Davy Jones is no friend of mine,
And that, up there in the lines, is that a winch,
Or a robot squirrel? The cold, the dark,
The long hours, they do strange things to a soul.

A SCREAM FOR THE SEA

Landlubbers!
Shipwrecks!
Grockels!
Ahoy!

Climb the masts!
In the brig!
Avast ye!
Ahoy!

Breakwater!
Saltwater!
Tidewater!
Ahoy!

Where are the giant squid?
Where are the dolphin pods?
Where are the lobster pots?
Ahoy!

And the trawlers
In their port
Look like giraffes
In the zoo
Ahoy!

Salt encrusted
Barnacle clung
Metal rusted hull!
Ahoy!

This long concrete arm
Protects us from harm
Calm our harbour
Ahoy!

We feel them deep inside
The tears of those who died
Washed ashore with every tide
Ahoy!

Weary legged trawler sailors
Bearded boat captains
Deck hands and net-menders,
Ahoy!

A bobbing anchored light
A rhythmic flashing sight
A beacon in the night
A buoy!

A prayer for the wind
Some salt for the soul
A scream for the sea
Ahoy!

HIVE OF ACTIVITY ON THE HOTTEST DAY OF THE YEAR

Welders and painters, sparks flying
From angle grinders, clouds of
Black exhaust, electricity generators,
Shouts and yelling and drilling and movement
And fork lifts and pick-ups and crates
Of fresh catch fish ice packed and
Unloaded as ropes are slung and
Boats tied secure and everywhere a motion
'Of individuals and yellow wellies and
Sweat brows wiped and amidst all
This toil unnoticed across the trawler
Basin entrance, a lone paddle-boarder,
Vain and so painfully superfluous.

WHY HAVE MOST OF THE BOATS GOT FEMININE NAMES?

Distant crews did opt for female names,
Jacqueline, Anne, Julie, Emily -
Mothering instinct instilled in inanimate steel,
A vessel protected, to watch over her children -
Offspring deckhands from the bully seas -
Or else a captain may cherish like a lover
The gentle caress of a remembered embrace -
Jacqueline, Anne, Julie, Emily.

MARGARET OF LADRAM LEAVES THE QUAY

A single blast from the horn
Echoes from the quayside wall -
Margaret of Ladram
Moves at a crawl,
Stately in her choreographed dance,
With a slow turn, churns the sea
And moves with a surprising ease,
This hulk of metal and rope and hope,
Yellow beams high like a surrendering thief.

THIRTY YEARS MAN AND BOY

For the sea creates sublime the mystery into which
A sprinkling of science and good knowledge of
Fish behaviour, patterns, historical trends and tides,
Like magicians, I am unable to divulge
The secrets at the heart of it lest less
Moral skippers may learn my methods;
Nonetheless let it be said that I often point my craft
Away from the fleet, tap into knowledge and
Then return with bigger loads; are you
Familiar with the methodology? And of course,
A hint of guesswork.

Thirty years man and boy, I've not done anything else,
Got my sea legs but even I spent the first six months
Spewing into a bucket, had to hide it,
Didn't want the others to think I was soft or
Not cut out for this, but the sunrise over the
Eastern sea when you stare up the Channel that,
Oh, that can lift you and it lasts all day, a
Bright sun over a flat calm sea and you just know
It's going to be a good haul.

In the dead of night in fluorescent glare I
Toil amid the flung sea spray salt lipped
In the inky boiling mass whose mystery is a
Locker that even the bravest dare not ponder,
Treacherous death washed with every foam-topped wave,
The craft itself rocking, you really don't want
To think of the dynamics as the nets slung each side
Reach down ever so into oblivion, there are
Mechanics at work here that can be
Truly frightening, you just don't want to think.

In a bed-warm slumbers my wife and kids and
While I envy their comfort, my toil makes it so,

Industry and sweat into eiderdown and a full fridge,
While those loving arms propel me forwards, further,
More exuberant, before beckoning me home that I
May regain my strength on the sofa surrounded by love.
What kind of amnesiac goes back?
But as I say, thirty years man and boy, and
The sea - oh, it runs through my veins.

SOLO SKIPPER

Just for a moment, when you're out there
With the sun and the gulls and the sea,
If you have time, you let out a sigh
And think,
'I am my own boss, master of my destiny.
I have grabbed the day and made it mine!'

I may be a solo skipper,
A crew of one on the smallest boat in the fleet,
But I'm part of something larger,
A passion that is in my blood and in the souls
Of everyone in this town whose livelihoods
And dreams are at one with the tides.

It doesn't really matter what I catch
So long as it's got eyes and an arsehole,
It's caught by me, from sea to shore and sold by me,
A lonely dot on the wild wide sea,
From net to quay,
Yes, master of my destiny!

Through winter squalls and the squawk of gulls
To the slap of waves on the bow and the hull,
Through summer sun and autumn fogs
To the warm embrace of this rock-clung port,
This sixty year-old sturdy machine
Purrs and throbs like a living thing.

When tides are rough and times are tough
And the day is an ache and you've had enough,
Tomorrow will be different,
The sea less belligerent,
And though I'm always vigilant I'll feel that sweetness
Deep inside enmeshed in belief

And the usual, eternal pride.

TRISTAN

He's the fella who owns the Adela,
All netty beams and a big propellor.
His catch is fresh, he's a quayside seller
To various chefs who only deal in stellar
Examples of fish.
He's a local Rockefeller
He's a Brixham dweller
His boat is his life, it's a tale like Cinderella,
If it's raining good fortune then
You'll need an umbrella
Cos he's the fella
Who owns the Adela.

ROUGH

We ride up,
Hold it there just for a second,
Then drop down, down,
Tingle in your stomach,
A grey angry foam-dotted wall,
The vehemence of nature,
How small we are.

I find comfort in the smallest things.
The sweep of the windscreen wiper.
No matter how precarious,
It keeps on sweeping.
It still does its job.

After a while you get into the rhythm,
Become at one with the sea.
It sets out its rules, and you obey,
Though every now and then
A freak wave, some dissonance,
A jarring note to make sure
You're paying attention.

And the old trawler, she
Creaks just like ships on films,
Juddering, straining, throbbing.
Hold on, here comes a big one.

You OK down there, cook?
He's bashing out an omelette.
I don't know how he does it.

GENERAL SYNOPSIS

There's a storm forecast.
Nobody's going out today.
Waves are crashing over
The breakwater.
The wind whistles in the beams.
It sounds like the Arctic.

In houses, cottages, living rooms,
Trawler folk drum fingers
On coffee tables as
Rain rolls down window panes.

Tied to the quay,
Metalk hulks bob on a swell.
Security lights gleam from
Wet concrete.
The fish pallets are stacked.
Everything is squeaking.

Plymouth, Portland, Lundy, Sole.
General synopsis
South-west storm force.

There's a storm forecast.
Wind blows the rain horizontal.
A shopkeeper stands in a doorway.
There's no-one around.

The trawlers.
They nod to each other
And share stories
Of rust and other ailments.
Tethered three abreast
In case they escape.

SUNRISE

You become used to the toil, the noise,
The discomfort, the salt-flecked waves,
The aching limbs, the diesel throb, the
Long hours, the constant motion, the
Tight space, and the sense of being at one
With a metal craft whose upkeep insures
Your very survival.

But the sunrise is different every day.

Heading East, into a myriad of colours, the
Night lightens with a halo, or maybe a red
Stain which bleeds ever upwards, or else
Resplendent yellow setting afire the water itself,
Or maybe through a swirling mist the sun
Will be a red circle rising with a mystical intent,
Perfectly round, or perhaps the day will just
Kind of start, and we'll be in the wheelhouse
And the skipper will say, come and see this, lads,
Come and have a look.

INTERVIEW WITH A TRAWLERMAN

Do you ever get tired of the physicality?
(Oh, the long hours, you mean,
The perpetual activity, the sea,
The lifting, sorting, winching,
The aching bones?)

Do you ever think of potential danger?
(Oh, you mean the mysterious depths,
The odd dynamics, the nets,
A broken beam puncturing below the waterline?)

Do you ever wish you were at home?
(Oh, you mean
Absolute comfort?)

Would you ever miss the canrarderie?
(Oh, the bonds that form, the jokes,
The shared belief, the adventures,
That friendly bunch of faces, the fact
That we all care for each other even when
We say that we don't?)

Do you ever worry?
(Oh, if only
There were time).

Do you ever feel at one with the sea?
(Ah, but does the sea ever feel
At one with me?)

Do you ever feel odd, walking on solid ground
After days on the brine?
(Oh, you mean that feeling of permanence,
Which is negated by the idea that time and life
Are always in constant motion, the ultimate example

State of the universe being chaos?)

Do you ever look at a fish and think, what on earth is that?
(Do you ever think they have similar thoughts about me?)

Have you ever seen a mermaid?
(Oh, you mean that old sailor's lament, the
Eternal wistfulness of the romantic mariner,
Mists curling in on a calm flat surface,
Drops of dewey moisture clung in his beard,
Wrinkled face pondering on better days,
Circumnavigators making up excuses for the
Slow madness of a life at sea?)

Do you ever sing sea shanties?
(There was that time in the Wetherspoons we all
Sat down and belted out It's Raining Men).

POET IN RESIDENCE ON A BEAM TRAWLER

Cod, halibut, mackerel, rainbow mullets,
Brown turges, narrow-eyes loomheads,
Grand flappers, suspended marlin,
Norwegian screamers, ribbon-tailed Kenneths,
Sole, turbot, plaice, haddock,
Bulbous flatfish, flounder, spasm ray,
Honey roasted dogfish, the common eel,
To name but twenty species of fish.
And scampi, that's twenty one.

And me? I think I'm gonna spew,
This old rusty tub flung round like
That Danish weather girl in the
Last series of *Strictly*,
Last night I honked up in my
Left welly
And only remembered this morning
When I put it on.

The trawlermen here have all got nicknames.
Stinky Sam is our captain,
I'd follow him to the ends of the earth, I would!
And Stinky James, our cook,
And Stinky Jim, who looks after the engine,
And Stinky Bill and Stinky Keith,
Who gut the fish.
These are the nicknames
That I've given them.

I was so cold last night
That my nipples went really big.
I had a weird dream
That I was stroking a caterpillar.
And in the morning Stinky Keith said,
'Gosh, my moustache feels really smooth'.

Oh, the banter!
This morning I was laughingly called
A *barnacle-encrusted puke-soaked*
Impertinent half-witted buttock,
And I said,
'Nice to hear from you too, Mum.'

Out on deck,
Hauling in a big load with Stinky Jim.
'Do trawlers often sink?', I yelled,
Above the clatter of the engine.
He replied, 'usually only the once'.

Gutting fish with Stinky Bill,
He's seen it all, has Stinky Bill
Looks one way, then the other,
And says,
'Sonny Jim,
Have you ever been sexually aroused
By a walru…'.
I said 'no.'

And a giant octopus stole my cheese sandwich
And a sperm whale
Tried to mate with us
And I was winked at
By a squid
And I'd never seen so many crabs!
And our captain was out on deck
With a jumping rope
Jumping up and down
I suppose that's why they call him
The Skipper.

And the sea got rough
And I spent the whole afternoon
Being tossed

As the trawler rose up
Through swell and wave
And the skies spat rain
They were ever so brave
This lonely tub
On the wide wide sea
Perhaps this was the wrong moment
To tell Stinky Pete
That he would make my life complete.

He slapped me
With a gurnard.

THE SEA MONSTER

Playing cards below deck.
Jack's got a good hand,
You can see it in his eyes.
Freddie's in the galley and he's
Clanging pots, the radio's playing.

And all the time the engine's throbbing,
Skipper Steve is in the wheelhouse,
He's been doing this longer
Than anyone can remember.
The new guy looks a bit green.

It's a squally night, said on a sea which heaves
Like the belly of a monk with trapped wind.
Our lonely vessel, the Unsinkable 2,
Was being tossed a-hither as if Mother Nature was
A bored teenager, and we were nought but a
Can of Pepsi
Idly thrown from hand to hand.

Of a sudden there came a crash and a splash and the
Slimy scaly suckered limb
Of a giant octopus
Smashed through the starboard porthole
And flailed around inside the bunks and sleeping quarters
Of the Unsinkable 2,
As tough Trawlermen gasped and flung themselves around,
Another scaly tentacle crashed through the door
And prodded and probed some more.
We were doomed!

At that moment our fearless captain, brave and courageous
Steve,
Clambered down from the wheelhouse,
Cried
Take off your shirts, lads! And line tight in a row!

That this briney beast may feel you with its accursed tentacles
And assume it to be the teeth of its natural predator,
The giant whale!
A natural reflex will cause it to retreat
Back to its ocean lair!

So we did as he bidded, each one of us
Bare chested and quivering as the tentacles slithered
Along our sweat soaked chests,
Then watched aghast as it let out a shiver
And just like Captain Steve had said,

Retreated back to the deep through the door and the porthole,
That we remained undefeated.

And jubilant cries rang out, never before did trawlermen
Jibber and tremble, their eyes lit with a sudden intensity,
That life may so quickly be plucked from them.
At that moment there came a ferocious knock on the starboard
Porthole
And with dread we saw the octopus there once more,
Watched dumbfounded as it
Reached in and left
The biggest toothbrush you've ever seen.

THE GHOST SHIPS

Through the mists of a calamity
In a year we never asked for,
The long arm of our shoreline bay
Offered you anchorage at first only
For commercial reasons.

Yet your streamlined sleek and tower block decks
Formed a fleet of imaginary towns,
Dark horizon Christmas trees with an
Imaginary population, new neighbours.

In a world of sudden restrictions you became
A local secret, an impossibility of the soul,
A solace as onerous as the mournful horns
Adding an extra solemnity for remembrance,

Seeing out this accursed year, or those
Poor fishermen who would never return.
We can sing sweet lullabies, dainty and plaintive
Though none can compare to your industrial symphony,

A blast of the horn as unsubtle as anything!
On foggy mornings you layer the imagination,
Ethereal in the gloom your hulking gross tonnage
A link to a world beyond immediate geography,
Ghost ships, haunting the present with voyages past.

IT'S JUST WHAT YOU DO IN THIS TOWN

'It's just what you do in this town.
I know more who've been out at sea
Than haven't.
I remember my old neighbour
Having a hospital appointment in Torquay.
It'll be the first time I've left Brixham
In forty-eight years, he said,
On something other than a boat . . .
The next time I guess
Will be in a coffin'.

THIS IS MY LIFE

I don't know how it started.
Did a favour for a mate,
Went out on his skipper's boat,
Liked the money
And before long it was just kind of assumed
I'd be there.
Fifteen years ago, now.
Been on three different boats.

It's not all work.
On that hot day,
That really hot day last year,
Millpond sea,
Skipper and the lads, we all dived in.
Weird seeing the boat
From the outside.

And my mate?
The one who got me into all this?
He don't do it anymore.
Works as a supermarket delivery driver.

I only wanted enough to buy
A place of my own,
A place for me and the wife.
And now,
This is my life.

SOMETIMES THEY DON'T COME BACK

Sometimes they don't come back

And the community
Close knit at best
Comes together.

A friend of a friend
Went to sea
And he never returned
And nor did his mate
And it felt
Like everything
Was closing in.

There's a statue on the quay,
Man and Boy.
It became a focus
And everyone left tributes.
This town
Has no secrets.

Flames flickered
In the autumn breeze
Under overcast skies.
Floral offerings
Heartfelt outpourings
The town
A shoulder.

And the grief
Never seems to go.
It's unimaginable.
You can't even begin.

Souls entrust in each other
That every boat which sales

Carries an extra presence
Acknowledged but never seen.

Because
Sometimes
They don't come back.

THE SKIPPER'S DECISION

In the old days
They'd come aboard
Worse for wear,
I suppose you could say.

Nothing worse
Than a hungover crew,
Mardy from the offset,
So I said,
Lads,
No drinking on board.

Which makes the first
Day or so
Particularly uncomfortable,
But they sober up.
They go through that zone.

Early in the morning,
Gliding past the stone breakwater,
They're very quiet.
And I am too, I suppose.
Coffee is OK.
Whatever else they'd need
To put a layer between themselves
And the world.

DAN

I'm a firm-chinned trawlerman.
I don't fight on the quay.
I'm not a brawlerman.
I don't stagger in the gutter
Getting legless in the pub
I'm not a crawlerman.
Although I'm not short,
I could be a bit taller man.
My name is
Dan.

Heaving seas much like the
Heaving bosoms of the girls I have
Pinned around my bunk.
In the middle of the night
In the midst of a gale I catch
Their slightly uncertain eyes in the glare
Of my mobile phone.
I've cut them out from magazines.

Yet my heart yearns and the
More it yearns I beg not
For a girl in every port.
The lessons I've learned,
The lessons I've been taught,
Someone to spend my time with
Because my trawler days are fraught
And my life will mean nought
Because I really ought
To find
Contentment,

Slippery nets as we haul in a big one,
Scales and flippers, kippers,
Frantic shouting from the skipper,

Diesel generators and lights
Illuminating horizontal rain.
How I tire of these
Seas
How I pine for a night
With a loved one.

I'm too old
For magazine cuttings.

Chugging into port,
A belly full o' fish
After a week on the big brine
Feeling an ache in every muscle,
A lonely room awaits me
Somewhere in this place, this
Collection of lights, this
Outpost of humanity,
This
Rock-clung town with its cottages
Like limpets holding on so
Tightly as if to an idea.

She's out there, I can feel
An untold story,
A future love.

I WANT TO BE A SKIPPER

I want to be a skipper,
I want to own a boat.
A twenty foot Dutch style craft,
To everyone I'd gloat:
'Look at me and my trawler,
It really is so smart!
With nets and spools and sonar,
It is a work of art!'

I'd call my trawler Percy
And then I'd hire a crew.
'Welcome aboard', I'd say to them,
'Kindly form a queue!'
And off we'd sail to fishing grounds,
Whistling as we go,
And come back just before sunrise,
Our faces all aglow.

I want to be a captain
In my wheelhouse cab.
Unloading at the fish market,
My word, it would be so fab!
Bobbling around in Percy,
Tied up in the quay.
I want to be a skipper,
It is the life for me!

DO YOU HEAR THE SEA STILL CALLING?

Sea-dogs and cabin-lads,
Cooks and schoolboys, cadets
And old hands with tales to tell.
It's so dark at one in the morning.
Do you hear the sea still calling?

A generation called to war,
A fleet depleted,
A country undefeated,
Patriotic employment,
U-boat periscope deployment
Seemingly without any warning,
Do you hear the sea still calling?

A metal spike broke the surface,
Gift from a silent foe this
Mechanical creature from the deep,
'Say your prayers, lads',
And every hand dare not breathe lest
An errant wave should draw it to the hull . . .
Detonate
Deploy
Smithereens
Heart-rates slowly falling,
Do you hear the sea still calling?

Tin fish on the high seas,
Literal minefields,
Sweepers and sleepers
Trawler nets a-haul
Souls entwined in brine
The ceaseless march of time
Trawlers keep on trawling,
Do you hear the sea still calling?

THE BATTLE OF THE EASTERN SCRUFF

The tin fish surfaced amid the Brownsail fleet,
A deep dive menace in manufactured metal so shiny and so sleek
Taking aim without a sound and peppering ships with shells,
Splintered jibs and sullied sails to sink to their watery hells.

Sometimes a soul acts braver than it ordinarily could.
The sea became a jumbled mess of ropes and sail and wood.
A bullhorn grabbed, a skipper yelled the first thing he could blurt,
'Stop it now, you silly fools, or someone will get hurt!'

Some boats made sail and hauled in nets, began to drift afar.
Others braved a hail of shells losing masts and booms and spar.
A boiler bursts with repeated hits spewing smoke and flame and steam,
A cacophony of tangled wrecks now circled the submarine.

Ship after ship disabled now, shrapnel and shot galore,
Broken decks and tangled nets this outpost of an uncalled war
Till all at once as if their thirst at last was suddenly sated
The firing stopped, the fishing fleet was torn and emaciated.

When hearts are strong and souls laid bare and fortune is a dance,
When fate steps in enmeshed with luck and quirks of circumstance,
Not a soul did waver nor for their safety choose to weep
A day which started normally now threatened with the briny deep.

Yet not a life was lost that day and of the boats only two,
Towed to port or rescued by their fellow fishing crew.
Welcomed home by onlookers limping wrecked and ruined and rough,
Wide-eyed men with tales to tell of the battle of the Eastern Scruff.

One hundred years and more have passed as I wandered on the quay
To ponder on this episode and such high-seas gallantry,
And tales of fortitude and pride and undoubted bravery

Of souls unwittingly tied forever with Brixham history.

MUM RULED THE ROOST

Mum ruled the roost.
Dad could be gone for up to ten days,
Chasing the fish and earning a wage,
She was strong.
Three of us to look after,
I don't know how she did it.

It was kind of assumed that we'd follow him,
Become trawlermen, and indeed we did.
We hardly saw Dad through our childhood,
Though I was the youngest,
I probably saw him more than the others.
He'd learned, by then.
And I tried it too, the trawlers.
Didn't like it.

There's a photo somewhere of my
Great-great-grandfather,
Selling fish down by the Prince William,
My Grandfather
In his wet fish shop,
My other Grandfather,
He came down from Rye.
Since the 1500s we've been
Making our living this way.

Imagine what it's like for a moment.
Beneath the hard exterior,
When the storms roll in there must be
Genuine fear, a husband
And sons at sea,
At mercy to the waves and the tides,
The inexplicable,
Good fortune, those twin propellers
Churning the water,
Miles and miles from land.

Mum ruled the roost.
Dad was always gone
And we knew he’d come home and spoil us,
Make up for it any way he could,
But it would be only too brief.
A couple of days,
And he'd be gone again.

THE FISH HAWKERS

Here we are, the fish hawkers,
Raised on brown sail soil,
We wives and daughters
Of endless toil, we,
Who cut and gut and pack the catch
Or in auction crowd we who aim to match
The hollored voices, we stand our ground!
Neither demure nor afraid to make a sound,
We, feisty fighty fishy folk
Hoist our barrels and foist fresh fish
From door to door to earn our keep.

We net menders, basket weavers
With tongues as sharp as butcher's cleavers,
Well-versed in lip, a comeback or three,
We speak our minds with liberty,
Let no-one doubt us, independent and free,
Strong willed and tough,
Does that scare you?

We fought for recognition,
More than cleaners or gossip gleaner,
We, who are slated for occasional misdemeanours,
The chance to match our wits over fish-packed barrels,
No strangers to fist-fights and neighbourhood quarrels
Stand our ground proud as any can.

Here we are, the fish hawkers,
Mothers of this town, keepers of the light,
Our voices echoing through cobbled streets
As we hawk our creels
For honest folk, for dinnertime meals,
Can you hear our ghosts amid the modern day trawlers?
We spirited types, we frequent brawlers,

Never silent, never ignore us.
Here we are, the Fish Hawkers.

LITTLE OSTEND

Send us your Belgians!
Not the usual rallying cry.
From Ostend they came,
Families and furniture piled
In a foreign fishing fleet
Welcomed by the town
In the middle of the night.

Shops were opened,
Bakeries into business,
Water taken to the quay
For these fisher refugees,
Whose home towns were
Quivering under the Nazi march,
And all was hopeless.

Over a thousand souls
A part of Brixham life,
In the shops and pubs and clubs,
Belgians whose knowledge
Of trawling methods was gladly accepted,
Belgians who became friends, and lovers,
And husbands and wives.

They served in cafes,
And schooled their children,
And plied their craft on trawlers,
Brixham, this Little Ostend,
This welcoming town
Proving that when humanity is at its worst,
It can also be at its best.

Take heed fellow humans,
That goodness will always prevail
And a heart will aim to share its warmth.
A town reaching out its fingers to another

Whose soul is in peril,
A trawler in a storm ,
The loving curve of the breakwater.

SQUIDBOX

Of all the buckets,
Containers, plastic tubs,
Amid forklift reverse hooters,
Shouting, throbbing
Trawler engines, plastic
Yellow coats, wellies,
High viz,
Of all the buckets
Of the aforementioned
None can be more repulsive
Than
The squidbox.

Deep sea dreams and
Night time beam trawlers
Dipping down on wave vales
Off the coast of Wales
With sonar and shouting,
Excitable as the net is
Brought up dripping
For commerce, there
Is no sport in this

And thence homewards
With a belly full of tubs trays
Buckets boxes profit gain
And rusty flanks from dripping nets
The loving embrace of a concrete
Breakwater.

The squidbox
Under fluorescent lights stark.

SEAGRASSES

Seagrasses
Underneath the ocean.
Seagrasses.
Poetry in motion.

They wave
With the waves
That's how
They behave
It's a seagrasses
Enclave
They're green
They got blades
They waves
With the waves

Seagrasses
Underneath the ocean.
Seagrasses.
Poetry in motion.

It's not
Hit and miss
I wouldn't
Dare to diss.
So much
Emphasis
On their photo
Synthesis

Seagrasses
Underneath the ocean.
Seagrasses.
Poetry in motion.

Yo yo sup? There's a seagrass bed
It's moving in the current its playing with my head
It's a natural protection it's a baby fish nursery
Sexy damn mo fo biodiversity
Say yo!
Say yo!
Say ecological and sustainable natural environment!
Got a place for the plaice go to pray for the ray
Got a ho for the roe get it out for the trout
Got a big fat puffer fish
See it on ma' supper dish
Big fat puffer fish
Would you like another wish
Big fat puffer fish
Oom wadda oom wadda oom wadda

Seagrasses
Underneath the ocean.
Seagrasses.
Poetry in motion.

Amidst their loomy meadows, oh look, the seahorse prowls
With its bitty flitty flippers and its horsey horsey jowls.
'Are you a seahorse?', I asked, he said, 'Nay'.

BIODIVERSITY

There are different fish, now.
Before, you could tell what would be where.
It's not like that.

Not that I'm complaining.
My buyers like a bit of the exotic.
You don't have to import
What's already here.

Often something comes up.
What's that?
We're all experts, now.
I don't mind at all.
But some of them find it
Slightly bewildering.

There's a colony of seals
In the harbour
And you regularly see dolphins.
That's nice.
It's much warmer
Than it used to be.

And some of the fish
You're not expecting to find.
Well,
You get a higher price
And everyone's happy.

It's disconcerting, though,
How much the
Weather is changing.

Have you noticed
There seem to be
More storms

These days?

I DON'T KNOW MUCH ABOUT MARINE BIOLOGY

I wish I knew more about mackerel
I wish I knew more about squid.
The secrets of the briny deep
Are something that have long been hid.
I stand upon the shoreline sand
I stand just inches from the sea.
I've learned so much in the life that I've lived
But not much marine biology.

I wish I knew more about flounders,
I wish I knew more about crabs.
Apart from their claws, they're no good indoors
And quite useless for hailing cabs.
I once met a marine biologist,
Please tell me, I said, don't be cruel.
In all honesty, he said to me,
Seen one fish, you've seen them all.

Don't ever trust a marine biologist
They're sneaky old and so- and-so's.
With their clipboards of facts and their waterproof macs
And their layers of warm woollen clothes.
I saw him that night at the harbour,
I saw him that night at the quay.
With a hop and a skip he jumped on a ship
And stuck two fingers up at me.

I'M A TRAWLER

I'm a tough floatie boater
With a proper prop and motor
I'm a hauler crawler trawler
I'm a total turbot-toter

I'm a clean pristine machine
With a spar and jib and beam
And a crew that's green and keen
If you know just what I mean

I'm a sonar blip daytripper
With a flipping chipper skipper
Catching cod and rock and roe
For a fish'n'chip shop flipper

I'm a drippy full-net winder
I'm a shoal of fish finder
And the load I brought in tuesday
Was a whopper and a blinder

I'm a bandit fish-stock robber
I'm a diesel engined throbber
And I'll keep you safe and warm
If you're wearing the right clobber

I'm a chuggy flounder lugger
In some foggy muggy weather
I'm a quayside harbour parker
With a strainy ropey tether

And you'll see me every day
In the ocean briney spray
And for my hunky bunky crew
I'm all they've got while we're away.

THE FISH MARKET HAS GONE ONLINE

The fish market has gone online
And with it, the soul of a town whose
Existence is built on danger,
Humour rejecting the obvious over these
Hard-won trawls, a place to display
The catch of the day
And to laugh, and joke, and josh, and gibe
And welcome home the weary crew.

Under white fluorescent lights
In an atmosphere so clinical as to
Bely the sweat and grime of its industry,
(Not like the old days when
They'd slam the fish down on the pavement),
A ballet of lab technicians these
Restauranteurs and dealers in their white coats,
White walls, white trays filled with white ice,
Even in this,
There was camaraderie.

The dance of figures tripping from the auctioneer's tongue,
A babble and confusion of numbers and percentage notations,
Earnest bartering, a price laid on each in
Humanistic terms, labour weighted and fortunes made public
Amid the gleam and sheen this raucous machine
Of social tradition and occasional profanity,
The eternal search for the highest bidder
Budgeted and boisterous and occasionally brave,
Face to face, seller, sailor, trawler.

There's a relief at the heart of it, each transaction is
Gritty in so many ways but greeted eye to eye,
A shake of the hand, a pat on the back, a grin, a smile,
A joke.
The only connection now is broadband.

The heart of the community is a click of a mouse.

ALL-NIGHT HUMMING FROM THE ICE FACTORY

At night I dream of the ice factory
Manufacturing glittered frost under corrugated iron,
Snow on cue, sleet on demand,
I dream as it chills the night for me
And glaciers the dawn.

Three in the morning, in sweated sheets
Flung aside!
Windows open and not a breath of air,
There's a humming noise coming from the quay.
What could that purring
Possibly be?

I'd like a snowdrift, please,
And ice so fine you can
See right through it!
I want to see my breath
In the trawler lights!

The sweat is rolling down my face,
And the hum, that's just adding to the
Intensity of it all,
And a throb of engines too,
The sweat is rolling down my face.
Don't tease me.
Freeze me.
be my icy queen!
Get me through this night!

At night I dream of the ice factory,
An ice conveyer belt and iced up workers,
Hauling ice and shovelling ice
And moaning about the cold.
Snow on cue, sleet on demand,
Blizzarding the morning as the sun rises

Over the trawler basin
And I moan and sweat as a clock strikes three.

I LIKE IT HERE

They cling to the hills like multicoloured limpets,
Slate tile roofs shining, fish scales reflecting
Sodium streetlights, the salt air
Curling in from a dark abyss.

This whole place is yours, right?
No, just two rooms on the second floor.

And is either of those a private cinema?
No, but you can get nextdoor's wifi in the khazi.

I like it here.
This corner of the universe.
I dream of escape
But I'll never leave.

I like it here.
It matches my soul
The centuries fold in
They embrace me.

I like it here.
So cosy here.
It feels I'm the century's daughter
Though I feel like a fish out of water.

I like it here.
I feel no fear.
I can be me here.

I like it here,
This is my home.
If only I didn't
Feel so . .

(Get a proper place)

I like it here
(Move on to another town)
I like it here
(Buy a mansion in the Hollywood hills)
I like it here
(Let me show you the world!)
I like it here
I like it here
I like it here

They cling to the hills like multicoloured limpets,
Slate tile roofs shining, fish scales reflecting
Sodium streetlights, the salt air
Curling in from a dark abyss.
I like it here.

WE ARE BRIXHAM

Amid the pontoons and jetties, the wind whistle
Through yacht mast rigging,
The stone breakwater a loving arm,
The harbour calm.
Amid the trawler bustle and diesel throb, the hum,
The roar, the continual movement,
Night-lights of long-distance trawlers
In their humdrum heroic return,
We are Brixham.

Amid the labyrinthine narrow lane cottages kissing
Face to face over alleyway cobbles,
Amid the crafty cats and shoals of sprats,
And bearded trawlermen in blue cloth caps,
Amid the grind and wheeze of autumn's first breeze,
Of chilled fingers numbed by winter's first freeze,
We are Brixham.

Amid the rust and plants and smuggling haunts
And quayside pubs where sea legs find their own solidity
On the moving deck of life itself,
Amid the gift shops and chip shops and ship hulls
And sea gulls and old father time his
Beard soaked in brine,
We are Brixham.

Amid the local lore, the drunk pub bore,
The concrete remnants of the Second World War,
The plastic floats, the high-viz coats,
The loaded totes from chugging boats,
The sea serene, the sea-scape scene, the holiday dreams
Of vanilla ice cream, the trawler beams,
The harbour walls, midnight pub brawls,
The pirate ghost ghouls, the mechanic with his tools,
The people, the town, the community and life,
We are Brixham

HOMECOMING

A lonely dot on a wild wild sea,
A nestle of rigs and beams, a mess
Of rust with nets slung low,
Giant spools and ropes slack dripping brine.

The hairpin concrete bend of jutted brick breakwater,
Of faded dead slow lettering, a test of time,
Scratched and blotched this tub sides a-slap
With the remnants of a sea bed scoured,

Hauled loads from sonar technology blips. At night
Each bunk holds dreams or high sea murmurs
As plastic macks drip dry, this metal tin
Of deckhand muscle, winches, graft, sweat.

They gain their sea legs, these sons and daughters.
A throb of diesel purrs the shuddering deck
And slantwise rain in a spotlight's glare,
Bow break waves and quayside forklifts, home, home.

www.ingramcontent.com/pod-product-compliance
Ingram Content Group UK Ltd.
Pitfield, Milton Keynes, MK11 3LW, UK
UKHW020418250726
13967UKWH00007B/2702

9 781445 718736